MG 6.0 2pts.

ESCAPING THE NAZIS
on the
KINDERTRANSPORT

BY EMMA CARLSON BERNE

CONSULTANTS:
MELISSA HACKER, PRESIDENT, KINDERTRANSPORT ASSOCATION;
LILLY MAIER, FULBRIGHT SCHOLAR

CAPSTONE PRESS
a capstone imprint

Encounter is published by Capstone Press,
1710 Roe Crest Drive, North Mankato, Minnesota 56003
www.mycapstone.com

Library of Congress Cataloging-in-Publication Data is available
on the Library of Congress website
ISBN 978-1-5157-4545-7 (reinforced library hardcover)
ISBN 978-1-5157-4546-4 (paperback)
ISBN 978-1-5157-4547-1 (eBook PDF)

Editorial Credits
Michelle Bisson, editor; Russell Griesmer, designer; Wanda
Winch, media researcher; Tori Abraham, production specialist

Photo Credits
Bridgeman Images: Pictures From History, 14 (bottom), Scherl/SZ
Photo, 16, SZ Photo, 18; Courtesy of Hans and Miriam Schneider
Family, 50, 86; Courtesy of Harry Ebert Family, 34 (all),
37, 40, 83; Courtesy of Jack Hellman Family, 70 (right), 75;
Courtesy of Kurt Fuchel Family, 24 (all), 27, 30, 32; Courtesy
of Tom Berman Family, 4 (all), 12, 80; Courtesy of Ursula
Rosenfeld, 60, 65, 88, Ursula's passport as design elements
throughout book; Getty Images Inc: Fox Photos, 76, Hulton
Archive/Topical Press Agency, 42, Universal History Archive,
59, UniversalImagesGroup, 14 (top); Granger, NYC – All rights
reserved/Scherl/Suddeutsche Zeitung Photo, 21; The Image
Works: Austrian Archives/Imagno, cover (bottom), 1; Newscom:
Europics, 92; Shutterstock: Chantal de Brujine, vintage white
paper background, emka74, vintage envelope (WWII) stamps,
symbols, LilGraphie, vintage photo frame/corners design, Nils
Z, cover (train), STILLFX, cover (ripped paper design), Studio
DMM Photography, Designs & Art, gold frame corners design,
THPStock, frames/edging design, zgj23, fabric texture design;
United States Holocaust Memorial Museum Collection, Gift of
Jack Hellman, 70 (left)

Printed and bound in China.
052017 010527R

TABLE OF CONTENTS

Tom Berman at age 4

Tom with his parents, Karl and Lenka,
in 1938, in Czechoslovakia

CHAPTER 1

TRAVELING TOWARD AN UNKNOWN FUTURE: TOM BERMAN

"The Leather Suitcase"

They don't

make suitcases

like that

any more.

Time was,

when this case

was made

solid, leather,

heavy stitching

with protective edges

at the corners.

Time was,

when voyage meant

train, steamship

distances unbridgeable

waiting for a thinning mail

weeks, then months,

then nothing

 Children's train,

across the Reich

stops

and starts again . . .

 Holland

a lighted gangplank,

night ferry to gray-misted

sea-gulled Harwich

again the rails

reaching flat across

East Anglia,

to London

 in my bedroom

the suitcase,

a silent witness

with two labels

"Wilson Station, [Prague]"

"Royal Scot, London-Glasgow"

Leather suitcase

from a far-off country,

Czechoslovakia,

containing all the love

parents could pack

for a five year old

off on a journey

for life.

—Tom Berman, saved by a Kindertransport

The fog pressed at the windows of the train screeching down the tracks. Outside, night lay like a blanket over the German countryside. The Nazis were out there. They had destroyed Jewish shops. They had shot Jewish men in the street. They had burned the great synagogues of Frankfurt. People were frightened. No one knew what would happen to the Jews of Germany.

Inside the train car, children leaned against each other in the seats, sleeping, mouths open, curled like shrimp in the laps of older brothers and sisters. Older children kept watch over little ones. Sometimes the fretful wail of a baby broke the rhythm of quiet breathing. The older child—who was the baby's only guardian—bounced the little bundle in her lap.

There were no parents on this train. Only a few adult volunteers had gone with the children. Those adults had to return to Germany as soon as the transport was complete. Once the train left the stations in Germany, no one else could get on. No one could get off.

Tom Berman was five years old. He was alone on the train, alone with the other children, who were also alone. Back in Prague, in Berlin, in Vienna, mothers and fathers were sad to have lost their children, but also relieved. They themselves were in danger from the Nazis but their children were safe because they had found places for them on the Kindertransport, which took children to safety.

All over Germany, Czechoslovakia, and Austria, trains loaded with Jewish children were pulling out of train stations. Jewish organizations had organized the transports. Priority was given to children without homes, orphans, and children whose parents were in concentration camps. The trains left from the major cities in central Europe: Berlin, Vienna, Prague. Then children disembarked at ports in the Netherlands, and sailed from there to Harwich, England.

German dictator Adolf Hitler was in power. He passed laws against the Jews. Germany teetered on the edge of war with the rest of Europe. Jews were not safe in their homes. They were not safe at school or at work. The Jews of Germany knew that they had to get out.

Aid groups in Great Britain tried to help. They pleaded with the British government, asking them to allow the refugee children into Great Britain. Then they had to fill out the paperwork necessary for the German government to allow children to leave. Both governments agreed. Germany wanted the Jews out of the country.

Britain rarely allowed refugees into their country, but they made an exception for children—with conditions. The children would not be citizens of Great Britain. Instead, they would be allowed in on temporary visas. They would remain refugees. They could not bring their parents. And when the war was over, they would go back to their families right away.

No one could know that when the war was over, there often would be no homes to return to. No parents. No families. Only the charnel houses that were the concentration camps.

The first Kindertransport arrived in Harwich, England, on December 2, 1938. It carried 200 children from a Jewish orphanage in Berlin that had been destroyed by the Nazis. The last transport from Germany left on September 1, 1939, on the eve of World War II. The last transport from the Netherlands left on May 14, 1940, just as Dutch forces fell to the German Nazi forces.

Back in the train, Tom Berman might have curled up on the train seat, his eyes squeezed shut, his hands clenched between his knees. A heavy, dark brown leather suitcase was jammed down in the space beneath his seat, perhaps. Around his neck was a string with a numbered tag.

Tom was very young. He had almost certainly never been away from his mother and father before. Tears may have squeezed their way from between his tight-closed lids. A lump in his throat too big to swallow would have

Tom Berman and his mother
before the Kindertransport

threatened to choke him as the Kindertransport train thundered its way through the night.

Tom is likely to have dozed and slept off and on through the night, and stared out of the window during the day. If he cried, there were only other children there to comfort him. Finally, the train crashed to a stop, the brakes squealing. The children crowded the windows of the train, pressing their faces to the glass.

They were loaded onto a ship and carried, seasick, rocking on the ocean, until they docked in England.

Tom remembers getting off the ship:

Night . . .

from the ship

a gangplank to England

sea smells rising . . . yellow lights swaying

line of labeled children

disembarking

from a darkening

Continent

—Kindertransport memory, June 1939, Tom Berman

Tom was perhaps carried forward along with a mass of children, crowding the dock, labeled with a number, breathing the free air of England—and waiting for the unknown future.

On Kristallnacht, an organized mob
smashed glass windows in Jewish-owned
storefronts and synagogues.

A Jewish-owned shoe store in Vienna,
Austria, that was destroyed by the
Nazis on Kristallnacht, Nov. 9, 1938

CHAPTER 2

FROM KRISTALLNACHT TO KINDERTRANSPORT

The crash of glass shattered the stillness of the night. A young man raised a club and, with one blow, smashed the glass storefront. The glass cascaded to the sidewalk. Then, with a yell, the mob of people surrounding him ran into the store, pulling down the shelves and throwing the contents onto the street. Up and down the street, the mob ran, meeting others, smashing glass storefronts and windows, until the streets were lined with broken glass, sparkling dangerously in the yellow glow of the streetlamps.

From the night of November 9 into the next day, November 10, 1938, groups of boys and men who supported the Nazis carried out of a series of pogroms, or systematic attacks, against the Jews. Some of the attackers were part of a group called storm troopers.

Others were part of a Nazi group for boys called Hitler Youth. Regardless of which group they belonged to, these

Horrified citizens watch a synagogue being burned to the ground in Berlin, Germany, during Kristallnacht.

mobs destroyed and burned more than 1,000 synagogues throughout Germany and Austria. They desecrated Jewish cemeteries and arrested Jewish men and boys.

Some of those set upon by Nazis were shot. Many others were beaten to death. Most of the other Jewish men and boys were transported to concentration camps.

In the end, more than 7,000 Jewish businesses were destroyed. So much broken glass lined the streets from the riots that the night came to be called *Kristallnacht*

(Crystal Night)—The Night of Broken Glass. This was the first time that the Nazis had systematically killed, hurt, and arrested Jews just because they were Jewish. But it would not be the last time.

Adolf Hitler had been the leader of Germany since 1933. He had been legally voted in by the German people. But gradually, he had become a dictator. That meant that he ruled over Germany and nearby lands by force. He made up any laws he wanted to. He did anything he wanted to people, and no one could stop him. The people who supported Hitler were called Nazis. They were members of what was formally called the National Socialist German Workers' Party.

Adolf Hitler and the Nazis believed that some groups of people should not live in Germany: mainly, Jews, but also gay people, people with disabilities, Jehovah's Witnesses, gypsies, and people who disagreed with Hitler's political policies, among others. Hitler and the

Following Kristallnacht, Nazi storm troopers rounded up and arrested local Jewish men in Baden-Baden, Germany.

Nazis invaded other countries near Germany: Poland, Czechoslovakia, the Netherlands, and parts of France. When they did, they started killing Jews, destroying their homes, and forbidding them to go to work or school. Eventually, the Nazis began sending Jews by the thousands to concentration camps, where, within a few years, millions were killed.

All over Germany and the Nazi-occupied countries,

Jewish people were afraid. They needed to get out of Germany—to leave, to flee to safer lands. After Kristallnacht, their fears were confirmed: Germany, their home, was no longer safe. But where could they go? All over the world, countries had closed their doors to refugees. War was coming to Europe. Everyone was preparing for it to happen. No country wanted to be stuck with thousands of poor, frightened people who were fleeing persecution.

Great Britain was different. After Kristallnacht, two large aid organizations, many other smaller ones, Quakers, and other individuals in England pushed their government to accept refugees from Germany. The two large organizations were the British Committee for the Jews of Germany and the Movement for the Care of the Children from Germany, later called the Refugee Children's Movement. They wanted to help the Jewish children of German-ruled countries.

The British government agreed to help. Great Britain would only allow in children under the age of 17. No parents would be permitted. Babies would be cared for by older children as they traveled. The government was wary of adults entering Great Britain with their children, then staying and trying to become residents. The parents might try to take jobs from British citizens, the government worried.

The British government also required every child to have his or her transport and care paid for by private citizens or aid organizations. The government itself would not contribute money toward the children's care. The aid organizations also needed to guarantee that, when the war was over, the children would leave. They were not permitted to stay in England once the danger had passed.

The aid organizations agreed. But the question remained: how would they get the children out of

Germany and the lands it controlled? It took massive amounts of organization. And it took the help of many, many people. Nicholas Winton, then

Two young Viennese girls talk on board the ship *Prague* in December 1938 on the way to placement in Harwich, England

a young stockbroker who was living in London, left his comfortable life to travel to Prague and help to organize the Kindertransports there. All in all, Winton saved more than 650 children.

Lola Hahn-Warburg helped set the framework for the rescue. Quaker leaders Jean Hoare and Bertha Bracey led a planeload of children out of Prague. Norbert Wollheim was a social worker in Germany who worked to transport the children out. Decades later, he recalled the arrangements in an interview with the United States Holocaust Memorial Museum:

So I took over . . . the responsibility for all

technical arrangements to be made in order to

bring the children out of Germany. The project

was 10,000 children, as I said. Now that was not

easy because we had no experience in this field.

The children were selected by [. . .] the welfare

organizations in the different cities of Germany,

and then . . . in a simple way they got their

permits, with the help of the English consulates.

[The] Gestapo (German secret state police), under

which supervision all of this certainly had to be

done, was very meticulous, they wanted . . . exact

records to be checked . . . so what I had to do was

. . . to not only prepare the records but also to see

to it that on a certain day on a certain morning

all these children were, were collected in Berlin,

for instance, where we had special . . . railway

wagons which would take them on the way via

Bergen, Hannover, to Hoek van Holland or

Flushing, and to Harwich in England . . . it had

to be organized in such a way that they all had to

come at a certain day at a certain time in order

to be ready . . . and we also had taken over the

responsibility . . . so that the police should not

interfere because certainly it was a tense situation

because the parents then brought their children in

order to . . . hand them over in to our custody to

. . . transport them to England.

The movement that brought the children out of Germany is now known as the Kindertransport. The children who rode on the trains were boys and girls, teenagers, and babies. They were Jewish mostly, but some were not. Some of their parents had fared well financially before the Nazis came to power, while others were poor. But they were all in danger. They all wore a number around their neck as a way to be identified and tracked so they wouldn't be lost.

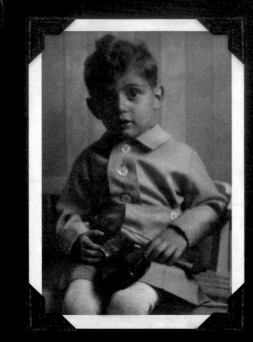

Kurt in 1934

July, 1933, Kurt and his
mother, Olga

Kurt and his dad

CHAPTER 3

A NUMBER AROUND HIS NECK: KURT FUCHEL

February in Vienna was cold and gray. Bare tree branches lashed the sky like angry skeleton arms. Kurt clung to his father's hand. Rudolf Fuchel was a big man, tall and broad. He was so strong he could stand on his head, legs pointing straight up. But Kurt's father could not pick him up and carry him out of the train station, as Kurt may have wanted him to. Kurt and his parents had to say goodbye to each other.

The train station platform was crowded, no doubt with frightened children clinging to their parents' hands. The air would smell of damp wool, leather, the soot of the steam engines. Breath would rise in white puffs, matching the thick steam chuffing from the train engine.

Kurt wore a number around his neck, a label printed on stiff paper: 386. That was who he was now. That was how those on the other end would know he was a Kindertransport child. His suitcase bore the same number. Rudolf and Olga, Kurt's mother, put their only son on the train.

Kurt pressed his face against the window, straining to catch a glimpse of his beloved parents. Rudolf shouted to his son to smile. Kurt managed to, though most likely he wanted to cry. At the sight of the smile, the Nazi soldier who was supervising said to Kurt's parents, "So young and already a hero." These were strangely kind words from a Nazi to a Jew. With those words, the train pulled out of the station.

The train journey was the beginning of a new life for Kurt, who had not yet celebrated his eighth birthday. Still, his world had been changing for some time. He used to live in a big, airy apartment in the center of

Vienna. He was the only, beloved child of his parents, who were gentle and kind, and had plenty of money. Kurt lived a peaceful life. Kurt's father was an athletic man who delighted in teaching his only child. Rudolf kept parakeets in their beautiful apartment. He would lift Kurt up in his strong arms and Kurt would watch the little birds pecking at seeds or tending to their chicks. Kurt went with his father to the public steam baths. In the winter, the family often went

Kurt and his father
enjoying the water together

sledding in the mountains, Kurt squeezed pleasantly between both his parents. In the summers, they went on beach vacations.

Rudolf was a manager for a branch of the National Savings Bank in Vienna. Olga, Kurt's mother, stayed home and took care of him. It was a blissful life.

Then, in 1938, Kurt's world fell apart.

The Nazis had taken over Austria. Hitler was in power, and now just being a Jew was a crime. Rudolf lost his job. His boss explained to him that he, Rudolf, had a "birth defect." The birth defect? Rudolf was a Jew.

Then his family had to move. And move again. Why? Kurt wondered, but he didn't know. After all, he was only a little child. He wrote about it afterward, as he understood it in his childhood:

> *"Times are bad," Mutti [Mother] says. Papa doesn't go to work any more, and he doesn't talk much. He plays with me, but he doesn't smile. I ask, "What is the matter? Was I bad? . . ." Papa tells me, "Times are Bad, but it will pass." In the evening, when I'm in my bed, I hear them talking quietly. They telephone a lot, they have important-looking papers on the table and the telephone book and a big map . . .*

I'm not allowed to go to my old school with my friends any more! I have to take the tram all the way to the end and then walk through some woods. The school isn't a real school, but a house. The class is in Herr Buxbaum's living room. All the big people furniture is pushed up against the wall, and we sit on little stools in the middle of the room. There are only ten of us and we are all Jewish . . .

Today the tram conductor said a bad word. He pulled the bell on the wrong side of the tram, so that it rang in the back instead of the front. The trams used to run on the left side, now they run on the right. I talk to all the people on the tram and tell them the bad things Herr Hitler has done, like telling Papa he can't work in the bank any more . . .

I can't go to school alone any more. People on

the tram were angry that I was saying bad things

[about Hitler], so now Papa takes me to school

and back home. We don't talk while we're on the

tram, but when we walk in the woods he tells me

that people will be very

angry if I say bad things

about Herr Hitler. "But

he is a bad man," I say.

Papa nods but doesn't

say anything . . .

Kurt's family had to move.

Then they had to move again.

A new law stated that any

Nazi supporter could take any

Kurt and his mother loved
being together

apartment that Jews lived in,

no questions asked. Kurt later wrote:

Frau Januba comes and shows Mutti and

Papa a piece of paper. I see that it has on it the

silly twisted cross and several stamps with pictures of a big bird, an eagle, I think. Frau Januba says, "This apartment is mine now." Papa is very angry with Frau Januba. He shouts, "How dare you take all we have worked for!" Frau Januba shouts, "If you say one word more, I'll have you sent to a concentration camp!"

[. . .]

One day Papa tells me that we are going to move again, but not together. He and Mutti will put me on a train and some nice people will meet me in a place called England, and I will stay with them for a short time and then he and Mutti will come for me. I like trains, but I ask, "Who will look after me, who will tell me where to get off, and why can't we all go together?" Papa picks me up and puts me on his knee. He says, "This is how it must be, and you have to be a good boy *and do what the ladies on the train tell you to*

do. You're not a baby any more, but a big boy of

seven."

Kurt became a refugee. So were all the children on the train with him. Wearing his label, Kurt rode the train from Vienna to Antwerp, Belgium. There, he and the other children were loaded onto a freighter ship, sailing for the east coast of England. All night, the ship

Kurt (right) with his
friend John in Vienna,
Austria

chugged its way through the black water, the waves slapping at its sides. Bunk beds lined the massive, dark hold where the children were tucked away like so many stowaways. Nurses watched over them and brought them warm tea.

In the morning the ship docked. England! Kurt might have swallowed bravely, squared his shoulders, taken a firm grip on his suitcase—and walked down the gangplank into his new life.

Harry at age 14, before
leaving home

Harry on his first day of
school, 1931

CHAPTER 4

A LONG WAY FROM HOME: HARRY EBERT

Harry had spent two days on a train. He was alone. His sisters had already left their home in Mannheim, Germany. In November of 1938, friends had taken the girls to live with a wealthy family in Holland. They lived in a huge house and attended the same high school as the future queen of the Netherlands.

Now it was January 1939. It was cold. Germany was on the brink of war with Europe. And it was Harry's turn to leave home. He was 14 years old. Harry's father was already gone: the Nazis had arrested him and taken him to Dachau, a concentration camp. Harry's Jewish boarding school near the city of Ulm had closed down.

Harry was used to packing for journeys. He had gone to boarding schools in other countries for years. The Kindertransport was just like those other journeys,

he told himself. Except that it was for good. Years later
he recalled:

>We first . . . took [the train] from Mannheim,
>then they had us stay overnight, either in
>Frankfurt, or in Cologne, I forgot. And they
>collected people from other locations, and they
>put them on a common train and took us into
>Rotterdam . . . at Rotterdam we stayed for a while
>in the quarantine station. That happened to—
>every port at that time had a quarantine station.
>. . . We could not leave, but we could have
>visitors. For instance, my sisters and theirs—and
>their foster parents . . . they came and visited me
>there. But we stayed in big barracks. There wasn't
>much to do.

If Harry missed his parents, he kept it to himself. He
ate biscuits with chocolate-butter. He ate lungen stew—
soup made with calf's lung. He was bored, as were the

Harry's sisters Ursel (left) and Lisel (right) in Holland, April 1939

rest of the children—there was nothing for them to do inside, and it was too cold to play outside.

Harry felt safe from the dangers of Germany. When he was sent to an orphanage in the town of Gouda, he even had something of a happy life.

In Gouda, we got involved with the town and its people. We played soccer against local boys['] teams, and we swam and skated at nearby lakes (but not on the same day). We even could get permission to go into town and to visit people over the weekend. I was very lucky and mobile

since my parents were able to send me my bike.

This enabled me to visit friends in the nearby

town of Bodegraven and more importantly,

my sisters, who were staying with a family in

Loosdrecht and were attending the well known

Werkplaats School in Bilthoven. . . . When biking,

I tried to hang on to slow moving milk trucks;

this illegal but common practice was less tiresome

and easier than peddling all the way.

Harry's life before the Kindertransport had been exciting and cosmopolitan. His father was an attorney and the family enjoyed great vacations. "My mother was great at us taking walks and hikes, and we used to go to . . . we used to go to the Heidelberg area, and went hiking into the mountains. And in winter I went there skiing with my father," Harry recalled in an interview many decades later. Once, he took the same train on the same day as Hitler himself, from northern Italy to Germany. Every town was hung with Nazi flags to welcome the Führer.

When he was almost 12, Harry's parents sent him to boarding schools in Italy, a luxury they could afford.

[It] was lot of good discipline. [When] you went to the dining hall, they checked your fingernails, so make sure they're clean. [We] experienced people from all over the world. They were not only Germans, they were also [L]oyalists from Spain who were fleeing after the Spanish—during the Spanish Civil War, which was going on at that time. And the school was very good, not too many students there . . . we got a lot of personal attention, and a lot of sports. We didn't have that much contact with the Italians, except we played soccer against them . . . I went swimming . . . There was . . . hard hat diving,

which is hardly done any more . . . in the bay,

catching squids and stuff like that . . . at dinner,

you were assigned to sit on different tables, and

at different tables, there was only a certain

language spoken.

Harry and his family in Holland, June 1939.
From left to right: sister Lisel, father
(recently released from Dachau), sister
Ursel, and Harry

Harry thrived at his schools in Italy. He loved studying. He learned French. He learned farming skills, along with the other students. They harvested seeds from eucalyptus trees and made oil. They picked figs, oranges, and lemons from the school gardens. Harry liked to eat the fresh figs the best.

In Gouda, Holland, in exile from his German life, Harry rode his bike. He studied. He visited his sisters. Would he see his parents again? Harry had no way of knowing. He could not be sure what the future held for him. All Harry knew was that life was peaceful right now. And all he could do was hope it would continue.

Liverpool Station, London, 1928. Ten years later, this is the station children would come into on the Kindertransport trains.

CHAPTER 5

THE IMPORTANCE OF A RABBIT'S FOOT: IRENE SCHMIED

Irene was leaving home. It was January 19, 1939, and she was 10 years old. The night before, she had run from room to room in her Berlin house, saying goodbye to each room, touching the walls, telling the house she would never forget it if she didn't come back. No one knew if she would return.

Irene joined a group of other children, all destined for the Kindertransport. They traveled to Hamburg, Germany. They were given lunch at a Jewish school. Irene had cocoa. It was delicious. Then the children boarded a bus to drive through Hamburg to the port. There, a ship would take them into their future. Irene had her doll, Peterchen. She had her memories. She had a suitcase. That was all she had—except hope. As she wrote later:

I glued my nose against the window and watched the walls of buildings along the street go by and the electrical trolleys glide past on their snow-covered tracks. Their bells tinkled whenever they stopped to let off people.

I turned to Marianne, [the girl] next to me. Did she have any idea where the bus was taking us? To keep the thoughts about my parents at bay, I tried to ask her why her father had not been at the station that morning. The right words would not come.

"Your Papi," I stuttered. "Is he at home?"

"Er lebt nicht mehr." (He no longer lives.)

She began pulling, almost tearing, at the identification tag hanging around her.

Even as I heard those words, so unfathomable to me then, there was a vague understanding of them deep within me. Years later, when we came across one another as adults in New York,

Marianne would tell me of the shot that had rung

out one evening shortly before New Year 1939.

The Gestapo had come back to fetch her father

even though he had only just been released—his

head shorn, his face gaunt, his eyes circled with

pain. Detained on Kristallnacht, he had spent a

month in Sachsenhausen, a concentration camp

near Berlin. Then he heard them pounding at the

front door again. He could bear it no more, and

had raised his gun to his temple.

In the bus that evening, I could find nothing

to say to her. The words "lebt nicht mehr" echoed

almost meaninglessly in my mind. I forced myself

to look out of the window at the street outside.

The row of shops along it sent its yellow light

out into the dusky air and onto the snow-swept

sidewalks. On this as on any other late January

evening, people stopped to point at the winter

sales displayed in the windows. Did they know

what was happening?

Finally the bus stopped in front of a long,

low brick building. Brown-shirted border guards

stood at the entrances. The light streaming out of

the barred windows hit my face. It sharpened the

pain above my left eye. The rabbit charm in my

pocket—a gift from my grandmother—began to

tingle between my fingertips. Leaving the bus, I

pushed myself forward to keep up with the others.

Instructions blared over the loudspeaker and

innumerable lamp bulbs on the long stretch of

low white ceiling blazed down. My suitcase grew

heavier as I inched my way toward the rows of

officials seated behind long wooden tables.

The voices, the rustling of paper, the smell of

dust and perspiration were dizzying. The glare

of the naked lights hit my forehead and prevented me from keeping up with Lottie, the social worker in charge, and the other children. Leaning against a nearby doorway, I waited for the pounding in my forehead to pass.

Opening my eyes again, I stepped into another place in the file. It was not the same line. A group of middle-aged couples surrounded me. Where had the other children gone? Alarmed, I thought of my parents. Would they be here? Were they still at home? I must find a telephone, to call them up, make sure that they were all right. The image of Marianne's father hit my mind.

The gruff voice of the official at the table jolted me back. "What is this child doing here?"

The people in the line turned to stare. I felt hedged in by a circle of questioning, anxious faces. They were all strangers.

The official turned to an assistant. I heard him say, "Get this child out of the way!"

The pain in my head seemed to burst. I took the rabbit charm out of my pocket and squeezed it for comfort. It was turning into a pulsating lump. The two customs officials were staring right at it.

A heavy tap on my shoulder sent a quiver through me and the rabbit plummeted to the floor. Not daring to pick it up, I turned my head, and found myself staring at the yellow scarf around Lottie's neck. She seemed ready to slap me. Instead she shook me by the shoulders.

"Come on, you should be over there with all the others on the Kindertransport line."

I held back and stooped to search for the little rabbit. I could not just abandon it amidst the dust, scraps of papers and cigarette ends that littered the floor. It was Lottie who saw its

glimmer, scooped it up and handed it back to me,
saying "Come on now, put away that silly little
trinket. Let's go!"

The rabbit in my hand once more, I saw how
tiny it really had been all the time. I stowed it in my
coat pocket, knowing that it was safe now. Taking
Lottie's hand, I followed her into the right line.

The smell of the sea drifted towards us as we
threaded our way through the crowd. In front
of us, a wall of lighted portholes of the vessel
stretched into the dark sky. I drew back. It seemed
as if a row of huge Berlin apartment houses had
floated down the river in pursuit. Or was this
still Berlin? Had I never left? Willing them
to turn back into the shining portholes of the
steamer [HMS Manhattan], I stared hard at the
cold bright lights. Then I grasped the railing, and
let the gangway pull me up into the ship.

Hans Schneider waiting for his flight to Prague at the Warsaw airport, November 1938

CHAPTER 6

STRANDED IN WARSAW: HANS SCHNEIDER

We received an order to leave this country

within 48 hours. This order was then changed; we

may stay until November 9. It would be our great

good fortune if the matter of Hansl were settled

by then. . . . We are infinitely grateful to you for

your efforts and I wish I could prove this to you

some day.

—Letter from Bella Schneider, Hans's mother, to Jacoba Coster-Lucas, member of the Dutch Committee to Help Foreign Children

In March 1938, Hans Schneider was 11 years old. He lived with his parents in Vienna, Austria. Bella and Hugo Schneider were both dentists. The Nazis had taken control of Austria. Bella and Hugo knew that their non-Jewish patients would refuse to see a Jewish dentist. The Schneiders would lose their livelihood.

And more than that—no one knew how dangerous the Nazi regime might become.

It was worse than they imagined. Soon after the Nazis took control, a man in a Nazi uniform showed up at the door of the Schneiders' dental practice. He told them that he was a dentist and he was going to take over one of the two examination rooms. It was legal for a non-Jew to take over any Jewish business or home.

Hans was struggling at school. Prejudice and discrimination against Jews were becoming worse. One day, the headmaster at Hans's school called all the Jewish boys out into the courtyard. True German children would no longer associate with them, he said.

Pay no attention, Hugo and Bella told Hans. But they could not deny—they did not try to deny—that the situation for Jews in Austria was becoming terrible. At this point, Austria was officially considered part of

Germany. There were more and more restrictions. More and more prejudice. More and more hate. Something had to be done.

Hugo and Bella were cautious people, but the time for caution had passed. At this point, before the war had begun, the Nazis hoped to drive the Jews out of their homeland. Jews were allowed to leave. However, if they tried to leave Germany they might not have anywhere to go. At this time, it was extremely difficult to get permission to enter another country.

Nonetheless, Hugo and Bella and Hans decided they had to try. In June 1938, they left their life in Vienna. They boarded a train for Czechoslovakia. They were now refugees.

This time, luck smiled on the Schneiders. Someone, somewhere, had bribed the Czech border guard. The train entered Czechoslovakia illegally.

* * *

Karwina, Poland

Dear Mrs. Coster, please don't be angry that I ask you to speed up the matter. Our situation here is so uncertain that I hardly know whether an acceptance that occurs only after a few weeks would still find us here. We are here completely dependent on our relatives who themselves do not know how their situation will develop in the next few weeks. That is why we would be so glad to know that our child has reached safety.

Should this matter be delayed for some time despite your kind efforts then it would help us greatly if you knew of a Dutch family in Poland (in Warsaw or elsewhere) who would be ready to keep Hansl until his departure.

—Letter from Isabella (Bella) Schneider, Hans's mother,
to Jacoba Coster-Lucas, member of
the Dutch Committee to Help Foreign Children

Hans and his parents went to live in Karvina, Czechoslovakia, with Hugo's brother. But soon, this part of Czechoslovakia became part of Poland. It was illegal for the Schneiders to live in Poland. Once again, the family was in danger.

Bella wrote again to Jacoba Coster-Lucas, who was a member of the Dutch Committee to Help Foreign Children. Could she find a place for Hans in Holland?

Bella wrote to Jacoba again and again. Her letters grew more desperate as time passed. At last, a place was found for Hans in a Quaker School in Holland. What's more, it was a school specifically for German and Austrian refugee children. Hans would be safe.

But first he had to get there. In October 1938, Hans and his father flew to Warsaw, Poland, to get Hans's visa from the Dutch authorities at the consulate there. Then, he needed to get to Holland without entering Germany. So he would have to fly on a plane to Prague,

Czechoslovakia. From Prague, he could travel to Holland, and to his school. Air travel in the 1930s was rare and expensive. Hans would be one of the very few children on the Kindertransport to travel this way.

* * *

First of all my heartfelt thanks. I can hardly

express in words how happy and grateful we are

that Hansl has been granted an entry permit

... [This letter then explains why Hans got held

up in Warsaw.] ... Hansl was intensely looking

forward to his getting out of here and it must

have been a big disappointment to him ...

—Letter from Hans's mother, Bella, to Jacoba Coster-Lucas

But, in Warsaw, the plane Hans needed to take to safety was grounded because of bad weather. When would there be another plane? Not for ten days. Hans could not stay in Warsaw—he and his father had no identity papers. They did not have permission to be there. They were in Poland illegally and if they were found out, they could be deported. If they were deported, Hans could not make it to Prague. He would not make it to safety. Hans was stranded and Warsaw was honeycombed with Nazis.

Hans and Hugo could not get a room in the hotel. No hotel would take someone without papers. They could not sleep on the street. Instead, Hugo grabbed the nearest neatly dressed man he saw. Speaking quickly and urgently, he explained that he needed to find a place for his young son to stay. Hugo did not know who this man was. He did not know if he would report them to the Nazis. He was desperate.

The man was kind. He sent Hans to stay with a diplomat at the German embassy. The family told Hans to say he was a relative from Vienna. Only later did Hans find out how close he had come to deportation. That man on the street had been a Polish police officer working in the department charged with deporting illegal aliens. With Hans safe at the embassy, Hugo made his way back to Karvina.

Why would the German embassy shelter a young Jewish boy? Why would the police officer work against his own department? Many years later, Hans could only guess that the police officer and the member of the German embassy were both involved with underground anti-Nazi resistance (those who fought the Nazis in secret). It was sheer luck.

Days later, Hans finally boarded the plane. As it rose into the night sky, he may have stared out the window, thinking of his many close escapes, of the luck that had helped him along the way. We can picture him wondering what his new life would be like. And if he would ever see his parents again.

A section of the eight-foot-high concrete wall encircling
the Jewish ghetto in Warsaw, Poland

Ursula Rosenfeld, known as "Ully" to friends and family, in 1948

CHAPTER 7

SHE NEVER FORGOT HER MOTHER'S FACE: URSULA ROSENFELD

Ursula Rosenfeld never forgot her mother's face, that summer day at the train station. Ursula was 14 years old and she was leaving—she had gotten a place on the Kindertransport train to England. She *must* go. Germany was no longer safe for Jewish children. But in the midst of all the chaos, all the pushing and shouting, being poked with the corners of others' suitcases, all the jostling and crying, Ursula must have seen nothing but her mother's face.

When she was an old woman, many decades later, Ursula told an interviewer,

The parting was terrible. That's the one thing I've never forgotten in all my life. And [my mother] had been so controlled. She'd always been

a sort of solid support to us and suddenly she

showed her feelings and it was terrifying, really

terrifying. You saw this face that showed all the

hurt and agony she'd been through. . . . I would

have liked to have had a happier image of my

mother. That's the only image, this contorted face,

full of agony. It's very sad.

We can imagine the train whistle blowing. "All aboard," the conductor might have yelled in German over the crowd of frightened children and weeping parents. Ursula memorized her mother's face.

The train was crammed with children crowded up against each other. The journey must have been terrifying. At the German border, the wheels slowed to a stop. The children sat up, murmuring and looking around. What would happen now?

Nazi border guards rolled back the door and stepped onto the train. They wanted to frighten the children. Ursula recalled, "The Nazi border guard very officiously came around, made some of the children open their suitcases. They shouted at us and threw their weight about."

When the guard left, one can imagine a collective sigh of relief among the children. And then the mood shifted. The train pulled out of Germany and onto Dutch soil. Years later, Ursula remembered:

> Not only were the frontier guards on the
> Dutch side very nice, they had a contingent of
> ladies who bought us cocoa and Dutch zwieback
> [sweet crackers]. And it was like manna from
> heaven, it was wonderful. We suddenly felt
> as though you'd been clad in a cloak of lead or
> iron and it had been taken from you. It was a
> wonderful feeling of freedom. We started to smile.
> I don't think any of them had smiled in a long
> time. It was wonderful.

Nothing had been wonderful in Ursula's life for a long time. Under Nazi rule, prejudice against Jews had been increasing. Ursula recalled that first time she realized she was different:

I was just about eight years old when Hitler came to power. I'd got some school friends and my mother always tried to make a birthday party for us. The table was set. I was sort of very excited. Nobody came. Not a single child came to this birthday party. That was the first terrible blow to me. I know it sounds trivial. But it was the first comprehension for a child to realize there was something different about you.

Oppression was closing in around the Rosenfelds. Ursula must have felt it because she recalled a strong sense of the horror that was to come. "I had had a strange dream in the night that my father was being arrested," she told her interviewer years later. "Our evening meal that evening that was the last meal I ever remember having with my father. I looked at him and thought, well I haven't really seen his features properly, and you know how you look at someone intensely. I looked at him and thought I should imprint his features in my mind." That meal was to be the last time Ursula would see her father. The next day, her world fell apart.

Ursula (right) with her sister, Hella,
around 1931

Our school happened to be just opposite on the street where the synagogue was. I was dragged out with a stream of children. Everybody went to the playground to watch these flames. And suddenly, someone said, "Oh there's a Jew, let's throw her on the fire as well." I don't know how I got home that day. I still don't know how I got home. And when I got home, my mother was absolutely shocked. My father had been arrested. My father was quite an outspoken person and so when they came to Buch[en]wald and when they took away all the men's braces and shoelaces, he protested and said "You can't treat these old people like this." So they made an example of him and they beat him to death in front of everybody in order to instill terror and obedience. They offered us my father's ashes in return for money. And eventually the urn came and we buried it in the Jewish cemetery but of course whether it was

his ashes, no one knows.

That day was the end of school for Ursula. It was the end of family life. It was the end of childhood.

The days that followed must have felt like a march of terror. The family sat *shiva*, the week-long mourning period, for her father, and then they found that the Nazis had stopped their bank account. Her mother could not get any money from the bank. They had only the food that was still in the house. They would have starved, except that people left them baskets of food. Ursula clung to these shreds of kindness. The world had not gone completely to pieces, then. Not if there were still people to bring them baskets.

The situation was becoming too dangerous. Ursula's mother knew she had to get her daughter out of their town. She sent Ursula to the Jewish orphanage in Hamburg, Germany, where her sister had already been placed. There, they would be safe. They could go to the Jewish school in Hamburg.

War was drawing closer to Germany, though. It was spring 1939, and Jews had to get out. Through the orphanage, Ursula and her sister learned that Britain's government had offered to take 10,000 children. Each child had to have a sponsor, though. Ursula had an uncle who, in 1933, had been able to escape the Nazis. He had been smuggled out in a coffin and had made his way to South Africa. He lived there now, in Johannesburg, and he had money. He would pay their expenses in Great Britain, if they were able to get on the Kindertransport.

Ursula's mother, alone in their town with her elderly mother-in-law, was thankful. The children would be able to get out and survive.

Ironically, though, it was her beloved father's violent death that saved Ursula. She told an interviewer, "In hindsight, I think my sister and I, we owe my father's death that we have survived, because they selected children who had a problem, who'd lost parents or whose parents could no longer look after them, to go on the Kindertransport."

On July 18, 1939, Ursula boarded the train. She kissed her mother and held back her tears. She turned her eyes to the future.

Jack's yellow bear

Jack Hellman, age six, on his first
day of school in Tann, Germany.
He is holding a traditional School
Cone filled with candy and gifts.

CHAPTER 8

CARRYING HIS YELLOW BEAR: JACK HELLMAN

A yellow bear lives in the permanent collection of the United States Holocaust Memorial Museum. It is a stuffed bear with a brown nose and it is labeled object number 2000.326.1. It was Jack Hellman's bear and it traveled with him when he made the journey on the Kindertransport from Frankfurt, Germany, to England.

Jack Hellman's parents gave him the bear when he was a boy in Tann, Germany. Before the war, before the Holocaust, before the Night of Broken Glass when the whole world changed.

The anti-Semitism in Tann was vicious in the early 1930s. Jews were not safe there. Jack remembered violent attacks:

I feared every day. I was just most unhappy going to school. I was walking on the street.

Six or seven boys came and called me Jew—

[expletive], then attacked me and threw me

through a plate-glass window. I was cut severely

and I had to go to the hospital for stitching. I

didn't want to go to school there anymore. I just

felt that I was threatened constantly.

Jack's parents sent him away, to the Philanthropin School in Frankfurt. The Philanthropin was a Jewish boarding school, the oldest Jewish school in Germany. There, Jack would be safer. He took his bear with him.

For four years, Jack lived in Frankfurt. He stayed at a hostel with other boys from the Philanthropin. Hugo and Lilli Steinhardt ran the hostel and took care of them. They had meant for the hostel to be an orphanage. But more and more well-off parents were sending their boys there to get them away from the violent anti-Semitism in the more rural areas.

But the boys could not escape the growing hatred

for Jews spreading through Germany. On November 9, 1938, everything changed. During Kristallnacht, people attacked the hostel where Jack lived. Jack remembered the morning after for the rest of this life. As an adult, he told an interviewer:

> I took my bicycle and went to school as always. There was no Jewish business that I passed that wasn't broken into. The merchandise was either on the street or looted completely. As I got closer to school, I saw huge pillars of smoke coming from the sections where the two big synagogues in Frankf[u]rt were. And I saw that they were on fire.

The massive synagogues were burned to the ground, along with the Torah scrolls and prayer books within them. And with that, Jack and the other Jews of Frankfurt had to go underground. Jack remembered years later:

My Bar Mitzvah was a month after Crystal Night. And it was held in an attic. My father was not there, my father was still in a concentration camp. It was just mother. I felt terrible. There was no celebration afterwards. There was nothing. You read your part from the Torah and you did your Haftarah and you were finished. And we were lucky that a minyan showed up altogether. I certainly felt the sooner that we could get out of Germany, the better off it would be. [After the hostel was attacked,] my housemother [Lilli Steinhardt] wrote to [banking giant] Baron James de Rothschild [in England]. Would he take twenty-four of her boys, her husband, herself, and her two daughters. And he wrote back in January that he would.

Jack Hellman left on the Kindertransport with the boys from the hostel, and Hugo and Lilli Steinhardt and their two daughters. With him, he carried a small suitcase, an identity label, and his yellow bear.

Jack (2nd row, 3rd from left) with a group of boys with whom he lived at the Cedars

Children on the first Kindertransport to

CHAPTER 9

LIFE AFTER THE KINDERTRANSPORT: THE CHILDREN'S STORIES

Many of the children of the Kindertransport went on to have long lives. Most were swept up in the war-ridden life of Great Britain during World War II. Tom Berman, the little boy with the suitcase, moved from England to Scotland to Israel, where he lived on a kibbutz. Later, he became a well-known professor of aquatic sciences.

Tom rode the Kindertransport one more time in his life—at the age of 75. A special commemorative Kindertransport train was organized. The train was a 1930s steam engine and passenger cars. Several surviving Kindertransport children—now elderly adults—rode it from Prague to eventually end in London.

TOM BERMAN

Tom was one of these, and he wrote the poem,
"Winton Train," about the journey:

Smelling again

the steam train smells

soot coming in the window

as we cross the landscapes

of the Czech lands,

woods and rolling fields

to Nürnberg

of dark memories;

the Rhineland-

and a choir of kinder

singing: Kde moj dom . . .

to Cologne;

along the level plains

of Holland

night crossing

to Harwich

with English gulls

screeching

as our train

pulls out of the platform

the Fens and

coming at last

steam wreathed

to Liverpool St. Station

Inspired by Good

a voyage reenacted

passing on the message

to a younger generation

So many stories

trajectories of lives

scattered

chance coincidences

punctuated

with jazz sessions

by the Hottentots

much laughter, tears

and a kaleidoscope

of memories shared

old friendships found

and new bonds made

Tom Berman holding the passport and
visa he used on the Kindertransport
at the 75th anniversary celebration,
held on September 4, 2009

—*Tom Berman, "Winton Train" (Sept. 1st-4th, 2009)*

Tom died in 2013 at the age of 79, after falling from a cliff in the Galapagos Islands in a hiking accident.

KURT FUCHEL

Kurt Fuchel went to live with a family called the Cohens once he reached England. Here, he recalls the first time he set foot in their house:

I remember walking into the house after the ride from Heroic [the port]. The image that comes to me is of a little boy [Kurt himself] dressed in his Austrian finery: short pants, jacket, long wool stockings held up by a suspender belt, and high-rising boots, the effect somewhat marred by the grubbiness accumulated during three days of travel. Ahead of me were the stairs going up to the second floor, at the foot of which stood [the maid] Salina who eyed me with obvious distaste and asked, "Do we really have to keep him? Near the top of the stairs sat John, a little boy of five, shyly looking at this new brother. Down to business: I was stripped, scrubbed from head to toe, my clothes burnt and new ones provided.

Then the family gathered around the table for a

magnificent chicken dinner. A smile returned to

my face. Here was a language I could understand.

Kurt spent many years with the Cohens, his English family, and kept in touch with them for the rest of his life. He fought in the British infantry during the war, and was reunited with his parents after eight years of separation. Both of them had survived the Holocaust. Kurt eventually immigrated to the United States and later wrote extensively about his experiences in Europe and England, including his time on the Kindertransport. He was one of more than 2,000 children who moved to the United States after the war.

HARRY EBERT

Harry Ebert was lucky too. His entire family survived the Holocaust and managed to immigrate to the United States in 1940. Harry fought in World War II as well, and went on to become a welding engineer. He lived a long life, dying at the age of 95 in New York.

Harry Ebert

IRENE SCHMIED

Irene Schmied never forgot the taste of the hot porridge with brown sugar that she was served on one of her first rainy nights in England. And she never forgot meeting her foster mother for the first time—a woman she quickly grew to love:

So now there I was on the platform, hugging my doll, Peterchen, waiting for a new chapter in my life to begin. A figure detached itself from the crowd and hesitatingly moved towards us, introducing herself as Pauline Muirhead. Her grey eyes sparkled with intelligence and there was an educated clip to her voice. Her loose tweedy clothes and the rosy shine of her cheeks gave her a countrified, unpretentious look that aroused immediate confidence in my mother. I also felt at ease and this made the parting from my mother less painful and the trip into the country more exciting.

Irene lived with Pauline and her husband, the philosopher John Muirhead, for almost seven years. Her mother made it to England as well, and in 1946, Irene and her parents moved to Chile. Irene moved to New York as a young woman, and spent her life in the United States, dying in 2010 at the age of 81.

HANS SCHNEIDER

Hans Schneider lived in Scotland during the war years. He believed that his parents suffered far more than he did in those years. "During the next five years we shared the experience of the British people at war, a remarkable people whom the world owes gratitude for their decision in September 1939 to fight Hitler. For a teenager, this was an exciting time; though I was an avid reader of newspapers, I did not realize the full horror of it until the war was over," Hans wrote years later. Some adult refugees were suspected of aiding the Germans—they were called "enemy aliens." Hans's father was one of the accused and was interned by the British on the remote Isle of Man in Scotland. His mother was forced to give up her work and live in one room with several other poverty-stricken refugee women.

Hans Schneider with his wife, Miriam, also a Kindertransport survivor

URSULA ROSENFELD

Ursula Rosenfeld remembered the joy of going to school. She told her interviewer, "We did start going to school [in England], actually, and it was marvelous. I'd never realized what school really was like, that you could participate. And I did enjoy school. And the wonderful part about it, it had a library. I waded through that library, and that's how I learned to speak English, really. And through that I got a love of English literature. But altogether it was a wonderful experience, and the children were so friendly to us."

Still, Ursula could not forget her mother. She needed to know where she was. "As soon as the war finished," she recalled, "[I] went to the Red Cross Committee and asked for them to search. Eventually, we got a letter from them to say my mother had been killed in Minsk, in Russia, where she was deported. It's very hard to come to terms with when you've always had that hope.

And of course, we've had no grave, really, no parting, no end, no funeral. It's that sort of vague feeling in the air of home, and that hope suddenly fading." That terrible, wrenching image at the train station was the last time Ursula ever saw her beloved mother.

Ursula and her family in 1964. From left to right: daughter Gill, son John, husband, Peter, daughter Ruth, Ursula, son Paul.

JACK HELLMAN

Jack Hellman lived a strange and grand life in England. He spent his days roaming the grounds of Waddeson Manor, the home of the Rothschilds. Jack also remembers being happy there:

> *My first impression of Waddeson Manor*
>
> *was it was like a dream, like a castle I've seen*
>
> *in pictures, but never, never seen anything in*
>
> *person. The Cedars was a servants' house . . . 26*
>
> *of us lived in the Cedars. The first thing we did*
>
> *was throw a soccer ball on the lawn and kicked it*
>
> *around. The local boys wanted to see what was all*
>
> *of a sudden being brought into their little village.*
>
> *When it was time for dinner, they said, "We'll see*
>
> *you tomorrow." I was so excited, I was absolutely*
>
> *so exuberant. I ran in to my housemother and*
>
> *told her, "Someone who is not Jewish wants to see*
>
> *me tomorrow."*

But Jack could not forget that his parents were still in Germany. He knew they were still in danger. And he was determined to get them out:

My father had a first cousin in London.

Every weekend I took the train into London and

bombarded him. I said to him, "Uncle Paul,

you've got to get my parents out of Germany."

And he said "I can't do it." After me being

so insistent, he finally said, "I'll give him an

affidavit if he has [a] working permit." I went

back to the Rothschild estate, knocked on the door,

and the butler, who was about ten foot six, came

out and looked at me. "What do you want?"

I said, "I want to speak to Baron Rothschild."

He said, "Wait here." I waited. After a couple

minutes, he says, "Follow me." I said to him,

"Baron Rothschild, my father's cousin will give

him and my mother a visa providing he has a

working permit." Without hesitation, he said to

me, "Would he work on a chicken farm?" I said,

"He'll do anything." He went to a notary and

made out a working permit for my parents.

It worked. Jack's parents made it out of Germany in the nick of time—they left the day before the war began. They survived.

Jack went back to Waddeson Manor in 1983. He was a middle-aged man then, and the traumas of the war were long over. But he wanted to thank Dorothy de Rothschild, the wife of Baron Rothschild, who had saved his life and the life of his 25 housemates more than 40 years before. Fifteen of the boys—now men— went to that reunion. Dorothy de Rothschild was 88 years old. But she remembered the boys clearly—and Jack was able to say what he wanted to say more than anything: thank you.

NORBERT WILLHEIM AND NICHOLAS WINTON

Norbert Wollheim and Nicholas Winton were recognized for their work saving Jewish children—they were called heroes, and Winton was given a knighthood. Wollheim died in New York in 1998 at age 85. Sir Winton lived to be 106 and died on July 1, 2015. A memorial service held for him in London's Guildhall in May 2016 was attended by 400 people, among them 28 of those he had saved.

Nicholas Winton with one of the many children
he rescued from Nazi Germany

But not all the stories of the Kindertransport children had happy endings. When the transports were organized before the start of the war, no one could imagine that 6 million Jews would be killed. The Kindertransport children knew their parents were in danger, but most people—the organizers, the families themselves—thought the families would be reunited after the war was over. And most of those people were wrong. Most children on the Kindertransport never saw their parents again—their mothers and fathers died in concentration camps, labor camps, in ghettos, or on the streets of cities and towns in Germany, Austria, Poland, and Czechoslovakia.

War took over Great Britain. Many Kindertransport children—then teenagers and young adults—joined the British military and fought for their adopted nation. Some immigrated to Israel or the United States. Still others had to endure another kind of trauma—despite their status as Jewish refugees, some were imprisoned in Britain as "enemy aliens." The British government was wary of anyone with a German background, Jewish or not, and swept through the towns and cities of Great Britain, spiriting foreigners away and placing them in internment camps.

Of the more than 10,000 children who came to Great Britain, about half stayed. Most of the rest immigrated either to the United States or to Israel. But throughout their lives, the children of the Kindertransport never forgot their German past and the Kindertransport that saved them. They called themselves "Kinder" —"children" in German—even when they were old men and women.

As a group, the Kindertransport children grew up to be very successful. Two of the 10,000 children won Nobel Prizes: Walter Kohn and Arno Penzias. And many of the children went on to work in helping professions. They were teachers, doctors, activists, and social workers. They had a strong desire to help strangers as strangers had helped them.

Altogether, the Kindertransport trains, boats, and planes directly saved more than 10,000 of the Kinder. More than 60,000 people owe their lives to the British Kindertransport: the children, grandchildren, and great-grandchildren of the Kinder all count themselves in that number.

Most of the Kindertransport children would never have survived the war had they stayed in their native countries. They were eight, ten, five years old. The children were rich, poor, middle class, and in between. They were boys and girls. Some were babies. They wore labels around their necks. They carried leather suitcases and waved their hands bravely at the station, boarding the trains that carried them away from their parents and away from their childhood lives. Six million Jews were killed by the Nazis during the Holocaust. One and a half million of them were children. But these 10,000 children lived.

—— 1933 ——

January 30 Adolf Hitler becomes Chancellor of Germany, bringing the Nazi Party to power

—— 1938 ——

March Austria is annexed by Germany in what is called the Anschluss, making Austria part of the German Reich

October Hans Schneider leaves Amsterdam and flies to Prague, then goes to Holland via the Kindertransport

November 9-10 Jewish businesses, synagogues, homes, and schools are destroyed in the pogroms later called The Night of Broken Glass, Crystal Night, or Kristallnacht

November 21 The British government approves the Kindertransport and agrees to allow German-Jewish children to temporarily enter Britain

December 1 The first Kindertransport train leaves from Berlin, Germany

—— 1939 ——

January Harry Ebert leaves Mannheim, Germany, by train on the Kindertransport

January 19 Irene Schmied leaves Berlin, Germany, on the Kindertransport

February Kurt Fuchel boards the Kindertransport from Vienna, Austria

March Jack Hellman leaves Frankfurt for Kindertransport, settles at Waddeson Manor in England

June Tom Berman leaves Czechoslovakia on the Kindertransport and arrives in Glasgow, Scotland

July 18	Ursula Rosenfeld rides the Kindertransport from Hamburg, Germany
September 1	Germany invades Poland, and the last Kindertransport from Germany departs
September 3	Britain and France declare war on Germany

—— 1940 ——

Harry Ebert immigrates to the United States with his family

May 14, 1940   The last Kindertransport ever leaves from Holland, just as the country falls to Germany

—— 1942 ——

The Nazis begin the systematic killing of the Jews in concentration (or, death) camps

—— 1945 ——

The Allies (Great Britain, France, the USSR, and United States) liberate the concentration camps, and the Nazis surrender

—— 1946 ——

Irene Schmied and her mother immigrate to Chile, where they join her father

—— 1951 ——

Tom Berman emigrates from Scotland to Israel, where he will live for the rest of his life

GLOSSARY

anti-Semitism—hatred of and discrimination against Jews

Aryan—a term used by Nazis to designate a supposed "master race" of non-Jewish Caucasians

bar mitzvah—the ceremony in which a Jewish boy officially becomes a man. The boy reads from the Torah in front of a congregation. For a girl, that ceremony is called a bat mitzvah.

charnel house—a building or room in which bodies or bones are deposited

concentration camps—a small area where members of a group are imprisoned against their will, and generally tortured, hurt, or killed

cosmopolitan—a person who has lived in and knows about many different parts of the world

desecrate—to damage a holy place

haftarah—a Biblical selection read during a bar mitzah, the ceremony in which a Jewish boy becomes a man

Hitler Youth—a Nazi organization for children and teen boys

Holocaust—the killing of approximately 6 million Jews by the Nazis during World War II, not counting 5 million others who were killed by the Nazis or who died in battle during the war

hostel—an inexpensive place to stay

internment camps—prison-like places set up to keep people during wartime

Kristallnacht—German term translated as Crystal Night. Also called the Night of Broken Glass, this term refers to the anti-Jewish riots and looting that destroyed Jewish homes, schools, businesses and synagogues during the night of November 9 and into November 10, 1938.

Loyalists—those who fought on the side of the democratic government of Spain in the 1930s

minyan—the group of 10 adult Jewish males needed to conduct a religious service

Nazis—members of a German political party called the National Socialist German Workers' Party. It controlled Germany from 1933 to 1945, harming and systematically killing people because of their perceived inferiority in race, religion, or other areas.

pogrom—a planned and organized attack on a specific ethnic or minority group. Governments often encourage pogroms.

prejudice—unfair feelings of dislike for a specific group of people

Resistance (also called Underground)—movements during World War II that attempted to fight the Nazis in countries the Nazi Party had occupied

shiva—in Jewish culture, a formal period of mourning lasting seven days

sponsor—to be financially responsible for

synagogue—a building used for Jewish religious services

Torah—the main religious text of Judaism. A Torah scroll is a roll of paper containing this text.

wary—not showing complete trust in someone or something because it could cause trouble

visa—a document giving a person permission to enter a country other than the one in which they live

THE KINDERTRANSPORT
— ASSOCIATION —

The Kindertransport Association (KTA) is a not for-profit, volunteer organization founded by Kinder and their children in 1990. The mission of the KTA is to locate, reunite, and bring together those individuals who were directly involved in the Kindertransport with those who have immigrated to North America and other homes, and their descendants. The KTA also educates new generations, as well as the public in general, about the Kindertransport's role in Holocaust history. The KTA also helps poor, parentless children of all races, religions, and ethnicities. To find out more, visit: www.kindertransport.org

READ MORE

Freeburg, Jessica. *Tangled History: Fight for Survival: The Story of the Holocaust*. Mankato, MN: Capstone, 2016.

Levine, Karen. *Hana's Suitcase: The Quest to Solve a Holocaust Mystery*. New York: Crown Books for Young Readers, 2016.

Steele, Phillip. *The Holocaust: The Origins, Events, and Remarkable Tales of Survival*. New York: Scholastic, 2016.

INTERNET SITES

FactHound offers a safe, fun way to find Internet sites related to this book. All of the sites on FactHound have been researched by our staff.

Here's all you do:

Visit *www.facthound.com*

Type in this code: 9781515745457

FactHound will fetch the best sites for you!

CRITICAL THINKING USING THE COMMON CORE

1) The British government required that every child on the Kindertransport be sponsored, or paid for, by an aid organization or a private citizen. Children who were not supported could not come. Do you think this was a fair arrangement? Why or why not? (Integration of Knowledge and Ideas)

2) The Kindertransport was organized after Kristallnacht. What was Kristallnacht and why was it considered a turning point for the Jews of Germany and Austria? (Key Ideas and Details)

3) Many of the stories in this book are told in the survivors' own words. How does this change the way we as readers experience the story? How would the stories be different if they were not told in the survivors' own words? (Craft and Structure)

BIBLIOGRAPHY

Berman, Tom. "Kindertransport Memory, June 1939." *The Kindertransport Association: Voices of the Kinder.* http://www.kindertransport.org/voices/berman_poem_memory.htm

--. "The Leather Suitcase." *The Kindertransport Association: Voices of the Kinder.* http://www.kindertransport.org/voices/berman_poem_suitcase.htm

--. "Winton Train Sept. 1st-4th 2009 (Kindertransport revisited)." *The Kindertransport Association: Voices of the Kinder.* http://www.kindertransport.org/voices/berman_poem_winton.htm

Ebert, Harry W. "Memories of a Kind in Holland." *The Kindertransport Association: Voices of the Kinder.* http://www.kindertransport.org/voices/ebert_inHolland.htm

"Former Kindertransport Refugee Calls on Cameron to Admit 3,000 Syrian Children." *The Guardian.* May 4, 2016. Web. http://www.theguardian.com/uk-news/2016/may/04/kindertransport-man-to-cameron-let-in-3000-syrian-child-refugees

Fuchel, Kurt. *Episodes and Fragments: A War and Peacetime Memoir.* Bloomington, IN: XLibris Corporation, 2008.

--. "Vienna, 1938: A Child's View." *The Kindertransport Association: Voices of the Kinder.* http://www.kindertransport.org/voices/fuchel_vienna.htm

Harris, Mark Jonathan and Deborah Oppenheimer. *Into the Arms of Strangers: Stories of the Kindertransport.* New York: Bloomsbury Publishing, 2000.

Hellman, Jack. *Into the Arms of Strangers.* Dir. Mark Jonathon Harris. Warner Archive Collection, 2000. Accessed via Amazon.com.

"Holocaust 'Hero' Sir Nicholas Winton Dies, Aged 106." *BBC News.com* July 1, 2015. http://www.bbc.com/news/uk-england-33350880

"Interview with Harry Ebert, October 16, 2010." *United States Holocaust Memorial Museum: Oral Testimonies.* Transcript of recorded interview. http://collections.ushmm.org/oh_findingaids/RG-50.030.0592_trs_en.pdf

"Kindertransport 1938-1940." *United States Holocaust Memorial Museum: Holocaust Encyclopedia.* https://www.ushmm.org/wlc/en/article.php?ModuleId=10005260

"Kindertransport 1938-1940, Oral History: Norbert Wollheim."*United States Holocaust Memorial Museum: Holocaust Encyclopedia.* https://www.ushmm.org/wlc/en/media_oi.php?ModuleId=10005260&MediaId=2488

"Kristallnacht." *United States Holocaust Memorial Museum: Holocaust Encyclopedia.* https://www.ushmm.org/wlc/en/article. php?ModuleId=10005201

Maltz, Judy. "World-famous Scientist From Kibbutz Amiad Found Dead in Galapagos Islands." *Haaretz.* April 18, 2013. http://www.haaretz.com/jewish/ news/world-famous-scientist-from-kibbutz amiad-found-dead-in-galapagos-islands.premium-1.516080

"Obit-Harry Ebert: Giants of Welding Industry." *A History of Welding. February 5,2014. Web. http://www.weldinghistory.org/whfolder/obit/obit-ebert-2014. html*

Nordheimer, Jon. "15 Who Fled Nazis As Boys Hold a Reunion." *New York Times.* July 28, 1983. Web. http://www.nytimes.com/1983/07/28/world/15-who-fled-nazis-as-boys-hold-a-reunion.html

Rosenfeld, Ursula. *Into the Arms of Strangers.* Dir. Mark Jonathon Harris. Warner Archive Collection, 2000. Accessed via Amazon.com.

--. *"Jewish Survivor Ursula Rosenfeld Testimony." USC Shoah Foundation. YouTube.com. March 22, 2012. Web. https://www.youtube.com/ watch?v=9ykVPLZzg2Q*

Schmied, Irene Katzenstein. "A New Home." *The Kindertransport Association: Voices of the Kinder.* http://www.kindertransport.org/voices/ schmeid_newHome.htm

--. "Departure (January 19,1839)."*The Kindertransport Association: Voices of the Kinder.* http://www.kindertransport.org/voices/schmeid_departure.htm

Schneider, Hans. "March 1938-August 1940: A Personal History of My Family During 30 Turbulent Months." *The Kindertransport Association: Voices of the Kinder.* http://www.kindertransport.org/voices/schneider_personalHistory.htm

SOURCE NOTES

page 5, "They don't make …" Berman, Tom. "The Leather Suitcase." *The Kindertransport Association: Voices of the Kinder.* http://www.kindertransport.org/voices/berman_poem_suitcase.htm

page 13, "Night…" Berman, Tom. "Kindertransport Memory, June 1939." *The Kindertransport Association: Voices of the Kinder.* http://www.kindertransport.org/voices/berman_poem_memory.htm

page 22, "So I took over…" "Kindertransport 1938-1940, Oral History: Norbert Wollheim." *United States Holocaust Memorial Museum: Holocaust Encyclopedia.* https://www.ushmm.org/wlc/en/media_oi.php?ModuleId=10005260&MediaId=2488

page 26, "So young and already a hero." Fuchel, Kurt. Episodes and Fragments: A War and Peacetime Memoir. Bloomington, IN: XLibris Corporation, 2008. Pg. 33.

page 28, "'Times are bad,'" Fuchel, Kurt. "Vienna, 1938: A Child's View." *The Kindertransport Association: Voices of the Kinder.* http://www.kindertransport.org/voices/fuchel_vienna.htm

page 30, "Frau Januba comes…" Fuchel, Kurt. "Vienna, 1938: A Child's View." *The Kindertransport Association: Voices of the Kinder.* http://www.kindertransport.org/voices/fuchel_vienna.htm

page 36, "We first…took [the train]…" "Interview with Harry Ebert, October 16, 2010." *United States Holocaust Memorial Museum: Oral Testimonies.* Transcript of recorded interview. http://collections.ushmm.org/oh_findingaids/RG-50.030.0592_trs_en.pdf

page 37, "In Gouda, we got…" Ebert, Harry W. "Memories of a Kind in Holland." *The Kindertransport Association: Voices of the Kinder.* http://www.kindertransport.org/voices/ebert_inHolland.htm

page 38, "My mother was great…" "Interview with Harry Ebert, October 16, 2010." *United States Holocaust Memorial Museum: Oral Testimonies.* Transcript of recorded interview. http://collections.ushmm.org/oh_findingaids/RG-50.030.0592_trs_en.pdf

page 39, "[It] was lot of good…" "Interview with Harry Ebert, October 16, 2010." *United States Holocaust Memorial Museum: Oral Testimonies.* Transcript of recorded interview. http://collections.ushmm.org/oh_findingaids/RG-50.030.0592_trs_en.pdf

page 44, "I glued my nose against…" Schmeid, Irene Katzenstein. "Departure (January 19,1939)."*The Kindertransport Association: Voices of the Kinder.* http://www.kindertransport.org/voices/schmeid_departure.htm

page 51, "We received an order…" Schneider, Hans. "March 1938-August 1940: A Personal History of My Family During 30 Turbulent Months." *The Kindertransport Association: Voices of the Kinder.* http://www.kindertransport. org/voices/schneider_personalHistory.htm

page 54, "Karwina, Poland…" Schneider, Hans. "March 1938-August 1940: A Personal History of My Family During 30 Turbulent Months." *The Kindertransport Association: Voices of the Kinder.* http://www.kindertransport. org/voices/schneider_personalHistory.htm

page 56, "First of all my heartfelt…" Schneider, Hans. "March 1938-August 1940: A Personal History of My Family During 30 Turbulent Months." *The Kindertransport Association: Voices of the Kinder.* http://www. kindertransport.org/voices/schneider_personalHistory.htm

page 61, "The parting was terrible…" Rosenfeld, Ursula. *Into the Arms of Strangers.* Dir. Mark Jonathon Harris. Warner Archive Collection, 2000. Accessed via Amazon.com.

page 63, "The Nazi border guard…" Rosenfeld, Ursula. *Into the Arms of Strangers.* Dir. Mark Jonathon Harris. Warner Archive Collection, 2000. Accessed via Amazon.com.

page 63, "Not only were the frontier guards…" Rosenfeld, Ursula. *Into the Arms of Strangers.* Dir. Mark Jonathon Harris. Warner Archive Collection, 2000. Accessed via Amazon.com.

page 64, "I was just about eight years…" Rosenfeld, Ursula. *Into the Arms of Strangers.* Dir. Mark Jonathon Harris. Warner Archive Collection, 2000. Accessed via Amazon.com.

page 64, "I had had a strange dream…" Rosenfeld, Ursula. *Into the Arms of Strangers.* Dir. Mark Jonathon Harris. Warner Archive Collection, 2000. Accessed via Amazon.com.

page 66, "Our school happened to be…" Rosenfeld, Ursula. *Into the Arms of Strangers.* Dir. Mark Jonathon Harris. Warner Archive Collection, 2000. Accessed via Amazon.com.

page 68, "War was drawing closer…" Rosenfeld, Ursula. *"Jewish Survivor Ursula Rosenfeld Testimony." USC Shoah Foundation. YouTube.com. March 22, 2012. Web.* https://www.youtube.com/watch?v=9ykVPLZzg2Q

pages 68-69, "In hindsight, I think…" Rosenfeld, Ursula. *"Jewish Survivor Ursula Rosenfeld Testimony." USC Shoah Foundation. YouTube.com. March 22, 2012. Web.* https://www.youtube.com/watch?v=9ykVPLZzg2Q

page 71, "I feared every day…" Hellman, Jack. *Into the Arms of Strangers.*

Dir. Mark Jonathon Harris. Warner Archive Collection, 2000. Accessed via Amazon.com.

page 73, "I took my bicycle and went…" Hellman, Jack. *Into the Arms of Strangers*. Dir. Mark Jonathon Harris. Warner Archive Collection, 2000. Accessed via Amazon.com.

page 74, "My Bar Mitzvah was a month…" Hellman, Jack. *Into the Arms of Strangers*. Dir. Mark Jonathon Harris. Warner Archive Collection, 2000. Accessed via Amazon.com.

pages 78-79, "Smelling again…" Berman, Tom. "Winton Train Sept. 1st-4th 2009 (Kindertransport revisited)." *The Kindertransport Association: Voices of the Kinder.* http://www.kindertransport.org/voices/berman_poem_winton.htm

page 81, "I remember walking into the house…" Fuchel, Kurt. Episodes and Fragments: A War and Peacetime Memoir. Bloomington, IN: XLibris Corporation, 2008. Pg. 34.

page 84, "So now there I was…" Schmeid, Irene Katzenstein. "A New Home."*The Kindertransport Association: Voices of the Kinder.* http://www.kindertransport.org/voices/schmeid_newHome.htm

page 85, "During the next five…" Schneider, Hans. "March 1938-August 1940: A Personal History of My Family During 30 Turbulent Months." *The Kindertransport Association: Voices of the Kinder.* http://www.kindertransport.org/voices/schneider_personalHistory.htm

page 87, "We did start going to school…" Rosenfeld, Ursula. *Into the Arms of Strangers.* Dir. Mark Jonathon Harris. Warner Archive Collection, 2000. Accessed via Amazon.com.

page 87, "As soon as the war finished…" Rosenfeld, Ursula. *Into the Arms of Strangers*. Dir. Mark Jonathon Harris. Warner Archive Collection, 2000. Accessed via Amazon.com.

page 89, "My first impression of Waddeson Manor…" Hellman, Jack. *Into the Arms of Strangers*. Dir. Mark Jonathon Harris. Warner Archive Collection, 2000. Accessed via Amazon.com.

page 90, "My father had a first cousin…" Hellman, Jack. *Into the Arms of Strangers*. Dir. Mark Jonathon Harris. Warner Archive Collection, 2000. Accessed via Amazon.com.

INDEX